Blue Ribbon Animals

SHOWING RABBITS AT THE FAIR

Gareth Stevens PUBLISHING

By Jennifer Wendt

Please visit our website, www.garethstevens.com. For a free color catalog of all our high-quality books, call toll free 1-800-542-2595 or fax 1-877-542-2596.

Library of Congress Cataloging-in-Publication Data

Names: Wendt, Jennifer, author.
Title: Showing rabbits at the fair / Jennifer Wendt.
Description: New York : Gareth Stevens Publishing, [2019] | Series: Blue ribbon animals | Includes index.
Identifiers: LCCN 2018030204| ISBN 9781538229316 (library bound) | ISBN 9781538232927 (paperback) | ISBN 9781538232934 (6 pack)
Subjects: LCSH: Rabbits--Showing--Juvenile literature. | Livestock exhibitions--Juvenile literature.
Classification: LCC SF453.7 .W46 2019 | DDC 632/.6932--dc23
LC record available at https://lccn.loc.gov/2018030204

First Edition

Published in 2019 by
Gareth Stevens Publishing
111 East 14th Street, Suite 349
New York, NY 10003

Designer: Katelyn E. Reynolds
Editor: Emily Mahoney

Photo credits: Cover, p. 1 (rabbit) JIANG HONGYAN/Shutterstock.com; cover, p. 1 (background photo) chainarong06/Shutterstock.com; cover, p. 1 (blue banner) Kmannn/Shutterstock.com; cover, pp. 1-24 (wood texture) Flas100/Shutterstock.com; pp. 2-24 (paper) Peter Kotoff/Shutterstock.com; p. 5 Juta/Shutterstock.com; p. 7 (English Spot, Holland Lop, Flemish Giant, English Angora, Belgian Hare) Eric Isselee/Shutterstock.com; p. 7 (Lionhead) photo-nuke/Shutterstock.com; p. 9 Lefebvre Alain/Shutterstock.com; p. 11 BIGANDT.COM/Shutterstock.com; p. 13 Photofusion/UIG via Getty Images; p. 15 Bobex-73/Shutterstock.com; p. 17 Laura Stone/Shutterstock.com; p. 18 Mel Melcon/Los Angeles Times via Getty Images; p. 19 PATRICK KOVARIK/AFP/Getty Images; p. 20 Michael Blann/Photodisc/Getty Images; p. 21 Helen H. Richardson/The Denver Post via Getty Images.

Printed in the United States of America

CPSIA compliance information: Batch #CW19GS: For further information contact Gareth Stevens, New York, New York at 1-800-542-2595.

CONTENTS

*Words in the glossary appear in **bold** type the first time they are used in the text.*

HOP TO IT!

Do you have a rabbit? Do you like to teach it new things? You can show your rabbit at the fair to learn more about rabbits and how to care for them. You can also find out about different types of rabbits, meet new people, and have a lot of fun!

With some hard work, you and your rabbit can enter the fair and maybe even bring home a blue ribbon! Read on to learn some basic tips about showing rabbits.

TAKE THE PRIZE!

A FEMALE RABBIT IS CALLED A DOE. A MALE RABBIT IS CALLED A BUCK. A BABY RABBIT IS CALLED A KITTEN, OR A KIT FOR SHORT!

Rabbits make great pets. They're also a lot of fun to show at the fair!

PICKING A RABBIT

If you already have a rabbit, you're ready to begin training. If you don't have a rabbit, you can look for a good **breeder** in your area. If you're lucky, someone in your community may be ready to give their show rabbit to a new trainer.

Havanas, mini lops, Dutch, and Himalayans are a just a few breeds, or kinds, of rabbits that are known for being good for young handlers. They're friendly and easy to train.

These are some of the different breeds of rabbits you can show at the fair.

ENGLISH SPOT

LIONHEAD

HOLLAND LOP

FLEMISH GIANT

BELGIAN HARE

ENGLISH ANGORA

GETTING COZY

Your rabbit will need somewhere to live. If you have an untrained rabbit, you'll want to have a **hutch**. The hutch should have a separate area for eating and be big enough so your rabbit has room to stretch out and move around.

A wire-bottom hutch can hurt your rabbit's feet, so you may want to put a piece of wood on the bottom. You can give your rabbit a blanket, straw, or a rug to sleep on. Clean your rabbit's hutch regularly.

TAKE THE PRIZE!

RABBITS LIKE TO SLEEP AT NIGHT AND DURING THE DAY, BUT THEY LIKE TO PLAY EARLY IN THE MORNING AND RIGHT BEFORE IT GETS DARK.

Rabbits like a cozy place to sleep, but they also need room to move around.

FEEDING TIME

You should make sure to keep your rabbit healthy. Just like you, a rabbit needs to eat good food and get plenty of exercise. Ask your **veterinarian** if your rabbit needs any **vaccinations** or special care.

Rabbits love to eat lots of fresh hay. They also need plenty of water available all the time. Being a **responsible** rabbit owner means feeding your rabbit on a regular **schedule** and keeping your rabbit healthy.

TAKE THE PRIZE!

RABBITS LOVE TO SNACK ON CARROTS, GREEN BEANS, CUCUMBERS, GRAPES, BANANAS, AND BLUEBERRIES. JUST DON'T FEED THEM TOO MANY OF THESE TASTY TREATS!

You can give your rabbit fruits and vegetables as a treat!

PRACTICE POSING!

The more you train with your rabbit, the better you'll both do in front of the judges. Working with your rabbit several times a week helps your rabbit get used to being handled and will help you learn how to position your rabbit to look good for the judges.

Read your show rule book so you know which poses your rabbit will have to do. If you're competing in showmanship, practice saying those poses out loud as you do them.

TAKE THE PRIZE!

SHOWMANSHIP IS ABOUT HOW YOU PRESENT YOUR RABBIT TO THE JUDGES. THE JUDGES WILL PAY ATTENTION TO HOW YOU HANDLE YOUR RABBIT AND HOW YOU BOTH LOOK AND ACT.

The more you handle your rabbit, the calmer it will be in the show-ring.

GROOMING

Grooming helps your rabbit's coat stay healthy. It also helps your rabbit to trust you. It's important that your rabbit looks its best for the fair, so take your time.

Some of the supplies you'll need to groom your rabbit are nail clippers, gloves, a soft cloth, and brushes. Set your rabbit gently on a carpet square before you start to groom so it doesn't slip. Your rabbit will be calmer if it feels safe.

TAKE THE PRIZE!

READ ABOUT YOUR RABBIT'S BREED TO SEE HOW TO CARE FOR ITS COAT. SOME RABBIT'S HAIR CAN'T BE BRUSHED BECAUSE IT WILL BREAK!

You may need an adult to help handle your rabbit when clipping its nails.

ARRIVING AT THE FAIR

It's time for the fair! Remember to bring your **registration papers** and check in once you arrive. Find the rabbit barn and the space you've been given for your rabbit. Be respectful of your neighbors' rabbits and pens.

Bring your own water, food, and bowls. Rabbits can be picky about different water and food. Keep your rabbit's pen clean and filled with fresh **bedding**. Check in often to give your rabbit fresh water and clean up any messes.

TAKE THE PRIZE!

TRY STUFFING AN EMPTY TOILET PAPER ROLL WITH HAY. YOUR RABBIT WILL HAVE FUN PULLING OUT THE HAY AND EATING IT!

You'll want your rabbit to look its best when people stop to see it.

HOP INTO THE SHOW-RING

When it's your time to be in the show-ring, don't be late. You and your rabbit should both be clean. Remember to smile and look the judge in the eye when you talk.

Be prepared to put your rabbit in the pose the judge asks for. Stay calm and have fun! Your rabbit will have fun, too. If you can, ask the judge what you did well and what you can do better next time. This will help you get ready for next year.

The judges will look closely at your rabbit.

GOING HOME

Showing rabbits at the fair is fun because you get to spend time with your rabbit and other people who like rabbits. Hopefully you'll be going home with a ribbon, but remember, not everyone can win. Be a good sport and **congratulate** the winner.

After the fair, clean your area and pack up your supplies. Thank everyone who helped you and your rabbit get ready to show at the fair. Remember to say good-bye to your new friends!

If you had fun, maybe you'll want to come back to the fair next year!

GLOSSARY

bedding: matter used for an animal's bed, such as straw, newspaper, or wood shavings

breeder: someone who keeps and cares for animals in order to produce more animals of a certain kind

congratulate: to tell someone that you are happy because of his or her success or good luck

groom: to clean

hutch: an enclosed area or cage for an animal

registration papers: an official record of information

responsible: having the job or duty of dealing with or taking care of something or someone

schedule: doing the same things at the same time every day

vaccination: a shot that keeps a person or animal from getting a certain sickness

veterinarian: a doctor who is trained to treat animals

For More Information

BOOKS

Brooks, Marigold. *Angora Rabbits*. New York, NY: PowerKids Press, 2018.

Murray, Julie. *Rabbits*. Minneapolis, MN: Abdo Kids, 2016.

Silverman, Buffy. *Dwarf Rabbits*. Minneapolis, MN: Lerner Publications, 2018.

WEBSITES

4-H
4-h.org
4-H gives children a chance to learn new skills through hands-on projects.

National FFA Organization
www.ffa.org
Future Farmers of America is an education-based organization for students interested in farming.

Rabbits
petrabbitcare.org/
Find information about how to take care of your pet rabbit here.

INDEX